KIRKE MECHEM

SONGS OF THE SLAVE

Suite for Bass-baritone, Soprano, Chorus (SATB) and Orchestra
based on material from the opera *John Brown*

SECOND EDITION

ED 3944
2d ed., first printing: March 2001

G. SCHIRMER, Inc.

DISTRIBUTED BY
HAL•LEONARD®
CORPORATION
7777 W. BLUEMOUND RD. P.O. BOX 13819 MILWAUKEE, WI 53213

NOTES AND TEXT

FREDERICK DOUGLASS is the central figure in this suite based on material from Mechem's opera, *John Brown*. Douglass, an escaped slave, became the greatest African-American leader of the nineteenth century; he was Brown's friend for many years.

I. Blow ye the Trumpet
(Chorus)

These are the words of John Brown's favorite hymn, prophesying both the day of jubilee and the martyr's death which Brown knew would hasten the destruction of slavery. What tune Brown knew for this hymn is unknown; the composer has written a new melody in the style of early American folk music.

Blow ye the trumpet, blow.
Sweet is Thy work, my God, my King.
I'll praise my Maker with all my breath.
O happy the man who hears.
Why should we start, and fear to die,
With songs and honors sounding loud?
Ah, lovely appearance of death.

II. The Songs of the Slave
(Bass-baritone solo: Frederick Douglass)

Recitative and aria. The composer has adapted the words from Douglass's autobiography.

My friends, you do me too much honor.
Music is my greatest joy.
Since I came North
I've been astonished to hear
That the singing of slaves is proof
That they are happy and content.
How wrong that is!
The songs of the slave
Are the sorrows of his heart.
He is relieved by them
As an aching heart
Is relieved by tears.

III. Dan–u–el
(Bass-baritone solo and Chorus)

The solo singer now represents an escaped slave. The scene is based on a real incident. In December, 1858, John Brown helped a slave family escape to Kansas from Missouri, then led them to safety into Canada. During that time, the mother gave birth to a boy whom she and her husband (the solo singer in this scene) named after John Brown.

Some of the words come from the spiritual, "Didn't My Lord Deliver Daniel?", others from the composer's libretto. The music is original but has the flavor of the great spiritual tradition.

DAN–U–EL
I'm free! I'm free!
John Brown delivered me.
Come on, you people,
Sing with me!

CHORUS
He's free! He's free!

DAN–U–EL & CHORUS
Didn't my Lord deliver Dan–u–el,
Dan–u–el, Dan–u–el,
Didn't my Lord deliver Dan–u–el,
And why not every man?
And why not everyone?

He delivered Daniel from the lion's den,
And Jonah from the belly of the whale,
And the Hebrew children from the fiery furnace,
So why not every man?
So why not everyone?

Didn't my Lord deliver Dan–u–el?
Yes, Oh thank you, my Lord.
So if my Lord delivered Dan–u–el,
Why not everyone?

DAN–U–EL & CHORAL RESPONSES
Now here's a verse, one more verse,
Come along and sing it with me.
You all know it's the gospel truth
'Bout how John Brown set me free.

Don't you know the man who delivered me
And saved me from the devil's livin' hell?
So I named my baby Little John Brown,
And changed my name to Dan–u–el.

CHORUS & DAN–U–EL
Didn't John Brown deliver Dan–u–el?
Yes, Oh thank you, John Brown.
So if John Brown delivered Dan–u–el,
Why not everyone?

IV. Dear Husband
(Soprano solo)

The text is an actual letter written by a slave mother, Harriet Newby, to her husband Dangerfield, one of John Brown's raiders at Harpers Ferry. Dangerfield was killed in the raid; his wife was sold to a slave dealer in Louisiana.

"Dear Husband:
Come this fall without fail.
I want to see you so much.
That is the one bright hope I have.
If you do not get me, somebody else will.
It is said that my master will sell me;
Then all my hopes will fade.
If I thought I should never see you again,
This earth would have no charms for me.
The baby has started to crawl.
The other children are well.
Oh that blessed hour
When I shall see you once more!
You must write me soon
And say when you can come."

V. A Speech by Frederick Douglass
(Bass-baritone solo)

Douglass was one of the great orators of his time. This scene takes place at a gathering of John Brown's family and friends, who have asked their newly-arrived guest, Douglass, to let them hear "the famous speech you made in England." Douglass was, in fact, enormously successful in raising anti-slavery funds in England. He was "a consummate actor who used all his powers of ridicule, pathos, mimicry and change of pace."

Most of the words in this "speech" are his own, but the composer has compressed and edited them from Douglass's speeches and writings spanning many years. The music is a dramatic combination of recitative, arioso and aria.

(with mock seriousness)
Ladies and gentlemen, I welcome this opportunity
To speak to you here in England.

What is American slavery?
Now most Americans do not want to hear this.
They love peace more than justice.
They condemn all talk of slavery;
They cry, "Away with it! It excites the Church,
Excites the Congress, excites the North,
Excites the South, the East, the West,
It excites everyone!"

Those who want freedom without struggle
Want crops without plowing;
They want the ocean without its mighty roar.
There is no peace without justice!

What is American slavery?
In law, the slave is the same as a beast.
He toils that another may live in idleness.
If a slave mother shall teach her child to read,
She may be hanged by the neck.
The whip, the dungeon, the bloodhound
Are all employed.
If slavery is right, then cruelty is right,
For one cannot exist without the other.

And what of the people up North?
Ah, they say to the slaveholder:
"We despise slavery, we abhor slavery,
We hate slavery! But if your Negroes run away,
We will gladly bring them back to you.
After all, that's the law.
But please understand: we hate slavery."

So much for the people up North.
They degrade us,
And then ask why we are degraded.
They close their schools against us,
And then ask why we don't know more.
They refuse to give us work,
And then ask why we steal.

And yet we are a hopeful people.
There is a vitality about the Negro:
Work him, whip him, sell him,
And he still lives and clings to America.
My friends, the destiny of the black American
Is the destiny of America.
The chain that binds the slave
Is tied to the neck of his master.

What do we ask of America?
Only that it complete its own revolution–
That revolution which declared to the world:

VI. Declaration
(Douglass and Chorus)

Douglass's speech leads directly into this setting of a portion of the Declaration of Independence. Brown's family and friends join Douglass, singing his words antiphonally, all coming together at the repetition of "All men are created equal."

We hold these truths to be self-evident,
That all men are created equal,
And are endowed by their Creator
With certain inalienable rights:
And among these are life, liberty,
And the pursuit of happiness.
All men are created equal. All! All! All!

Important Notice

Performances of this work must be licensed by the publisher.

All inquiries should be directed to the Publisher:

G. Schirmer Rental Library
445 Bellvale Road, Box 572
Chester, NY 10918
(845) 469–2271

First performance: June 12, 1994, First Methodist Church,
the Santa Monica College Concert Chorale
with the Los Angeles Concert Orchestra, James E. Smith, conductor.

duration: ca. 34 minutes

performance material is available on rental from the publisher

(original instrumentation: 3333 4331 Timpani, 4 Percussion players, Harp, Strings)
(reduced instrumentation: 2222 4220 Timpani, 2 Percussion players, Harp, Strings)

commissioned by the Don and Beverley Carlson Music Fund for the First United Methodist Church,
the Santa Monica College Concert Chorale and the Los Angeles Concert Orchestra, Dr. James E. Smith, conductor

SONGS OF THE SLAVE

I. Blow Ye the Trumpet

Kirke Mechem
Op. 51b

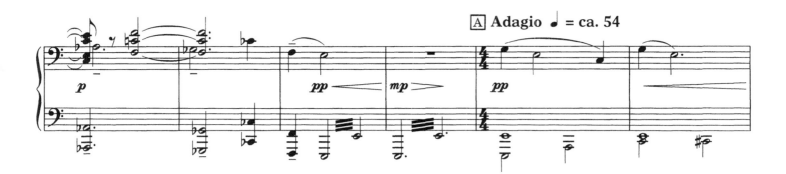

poco accel.   **B** **Andante sostenuto** ♩ = ca. 66

poco rall.   **C** **Adagio** ♩ = 54

D **Andante sostenuto** ♩ = 66

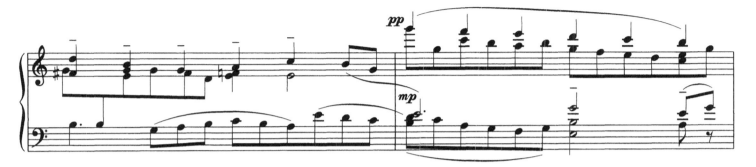

poco animando poco a poco

E **Allegro** ♩. = 60

pochissimo rallentando

4

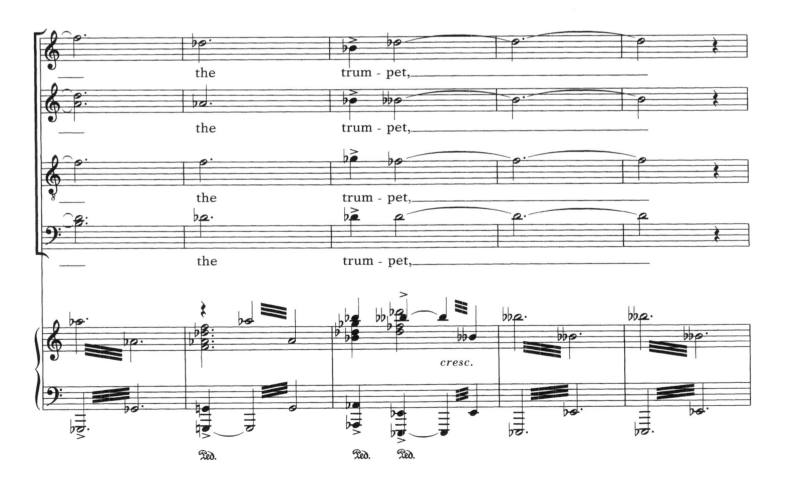

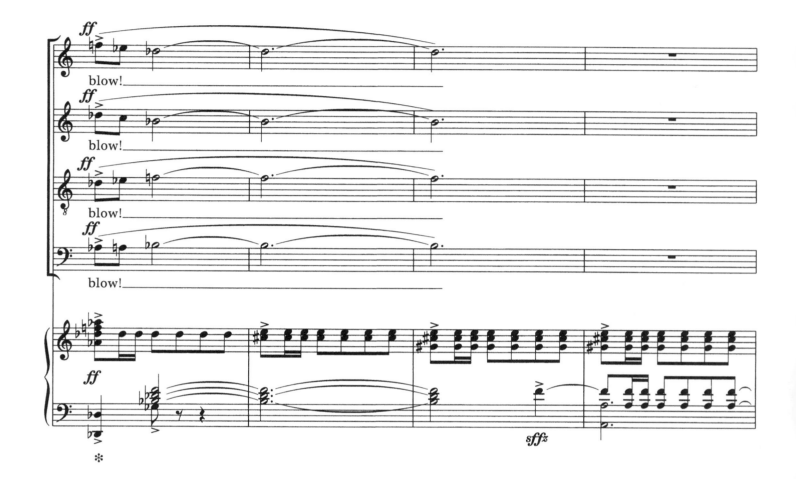

blow!

blow!

blow!

blow!

pochissimo rallentando

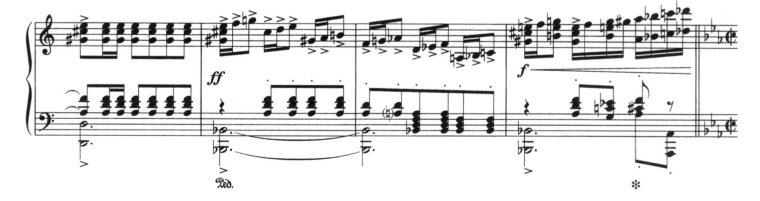

1 **Poco più animato (ma non troppo)**

Poco più animato (ma non troppo)

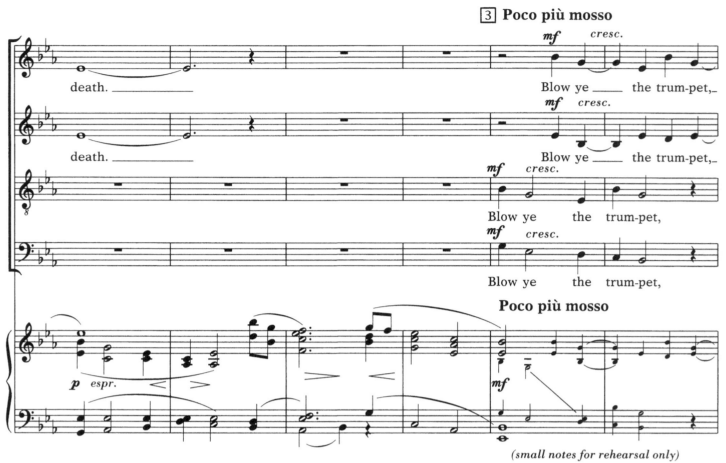

3 Poco più mosso

(small notes for rehearsal only)

Why_ should we fear __ to _ die, With_ songs __ and hon-ors sound-ing loud? __

should we start __ and fear to _ die, With songs __ and hon-ors sound-ing loud? __

Why_ fear to _ die, With_ songs and hon-ors sound-ing loud? __

Why_ should_ we fear to die, With songs __ and hon-ors sound-ing loud? __

5 **Tempo I**

poco rall.

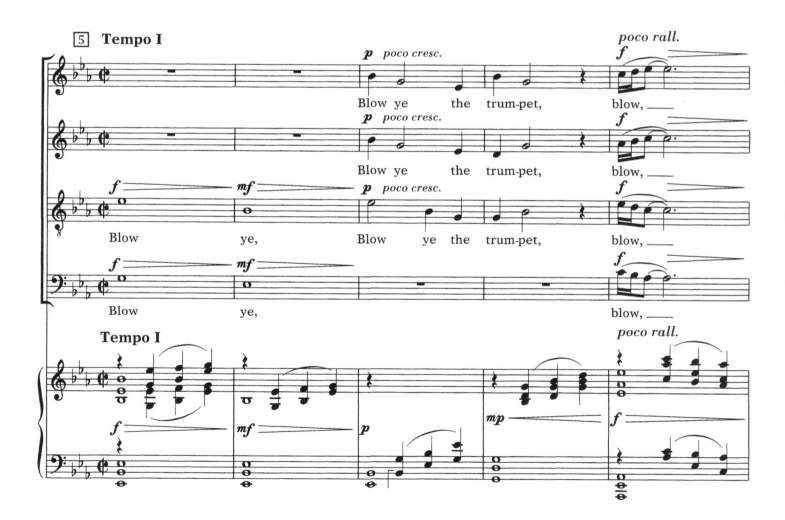

Blow ye the trum-pet, blow, ____

Blow ye the trum-pet, blow, ____

Blow ye, Blow ye the trum-pet, blow, ____

Blow ye, blow, ____

Tempo I

poco rall.

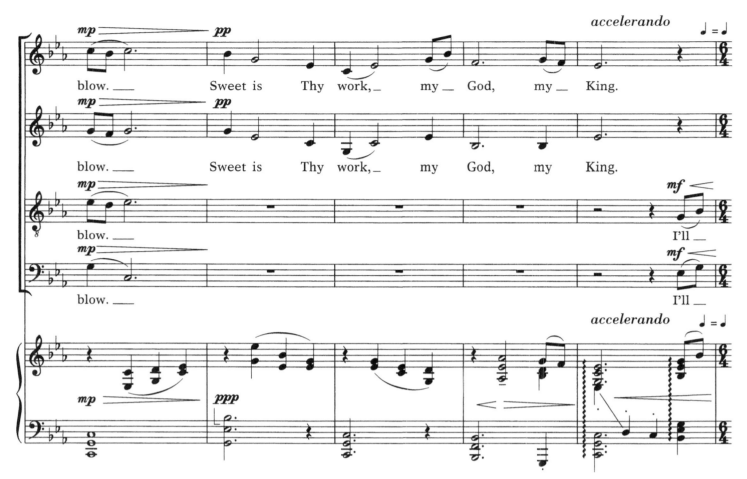

6 **Più mosso** ♩ = 120 (♩. = 40)

II. The Songs of the Slave

Adagio, poco rubato ♩ = ca. 54

Frederick Douglass

My friends, you do me too much hon-or.__ Mu-sic is my great - est

joy. _____ Since I came North, I've been as-ton-ished to hear that the sing-ing of slaves is

ritenuto　　　　　*a tempo*　　　　　　　　*rall. poco a poco*

proof that they are hap-py and con - tent. _____ How wrong that is! How wrong!

1 **Sostenuto** ♩ = ca. 63　　*p*

The songs of the slave are the sor-rows of his

una corda

heart, _____ the sor-rows of his heart. _____ The

2 poco a poco

songs of the slave are the sor - rows, sor-rows of his heart. __

3

He is re - lieved by them as an ach - - ing, ach - ing heart _

is re-lieved _____ by tears, an ach-ing, ach-ing heart _____

_____ is re-lieved by tears, _____ by tears. _____ The

songs of the slave are the sor-rows of his heart, _____ the sor - - - rows

of his heart. _____

III. Dan–u–el

* "Didn't," although always notated as a single syllable, should be sung as two syllables:

Did-n't

* "Didn't," although always notated as a single syllable, should be sung as two syllables: ♪♩
Did-n't

10

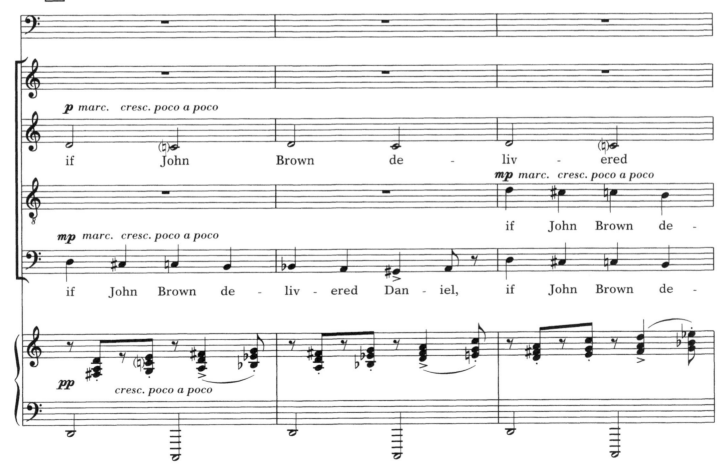

* The cue-size notes may be taken by Soprano I *instead* of the upper part written in normal-size notes.

IV. Dear Husband

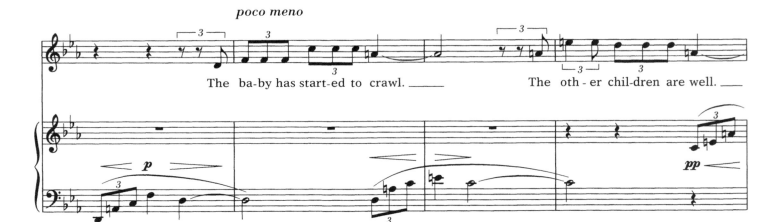

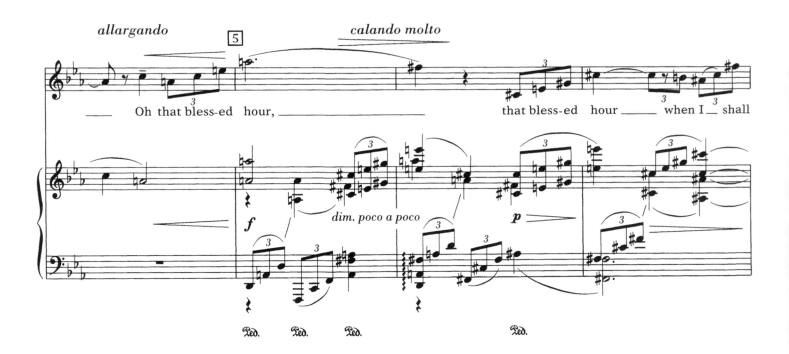

V. A Speech by Frederick Douglass

poco rit.　　a piacere　　2 a tempo

What is ___ A-mer-i-can slave-ry?

ff　　　　　p　col canto　p　molto

f　sffz　sffz　sffz　sffz　ff

3 Meno mosso ♩ = 104　　　　poco animando

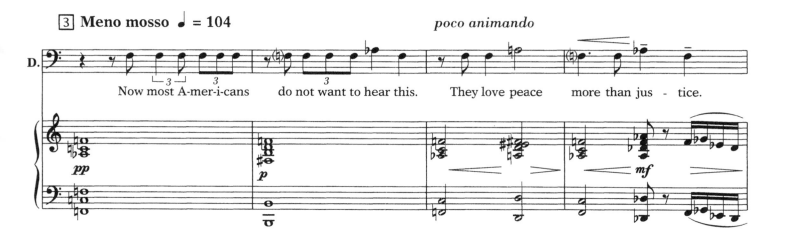

D.

Now most A-mer-i-cans　do not want to hear this.　They love peace　more than jus - tice.

pp　p　mf

accelerando
cresc.

They con-demn all talk　of slav-er-y; ___　they cry, "A - way with it!　A - way　with

p　cresc.　f

plow - ing;   they want the o - cean   with - out   its might - y

roar.

There   is   no   peace,   there

is   no   peace   with-out   jus - tice!

What is ___ A-mer-i-can

8 **Sostenuto** (♩ = 54)

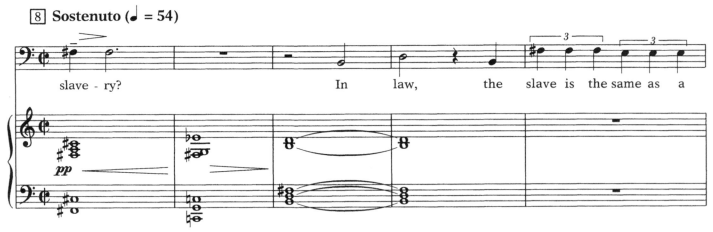

slave - ry? In law, the slave is the same as a

9

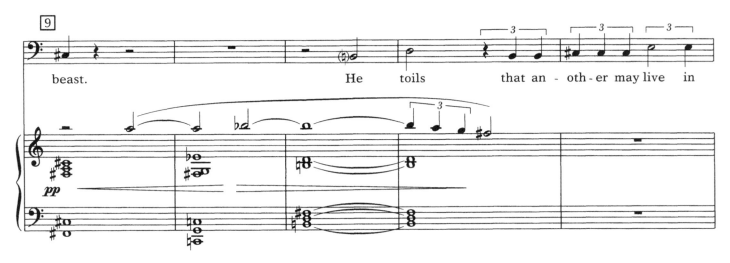

beast. He toils that an - oth-er may live in

id - le-ness. If a slave moth-er shall teach her child to

poco rall.

rit. a piacere
mockingly sweet
dim.

And what of the peo-ple up North? Ah, _____ they say to the

col canto

13 *a tempo*

risoluto   cresc.   f

slave-hold-er: "We de - spise   slave-ry,   ab - hor   slave-ry,   we

cresc. poco a poco

ritenuto   p

hate _____   slave - ry!   But if your

14   a tempo   ritard.   p sweetly sarcastic
cresc.

Ne-groes run   a - way, _____   we will glad - ly bring them

ppp
cresc.

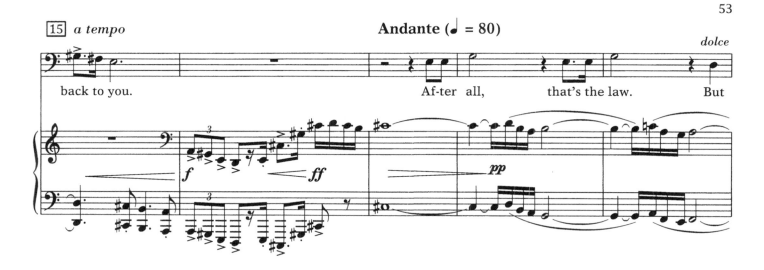

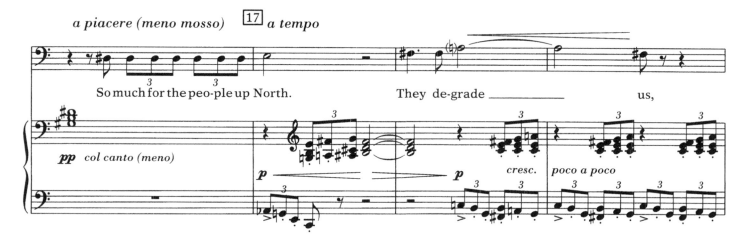

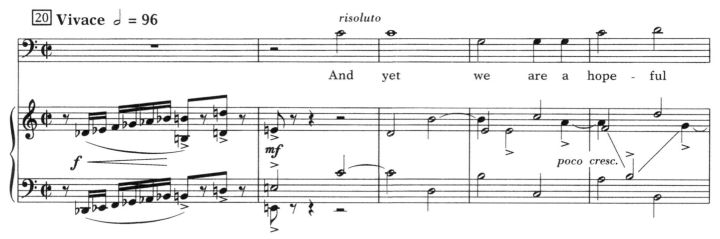

20 **Vivace** ♩ = 96 *risoluto*

And yet we are a hope - ful

21

peo - ple. There is a vi - tal - i - ty

22

a - bout the Ne - gro: work him, whip him, sell him,

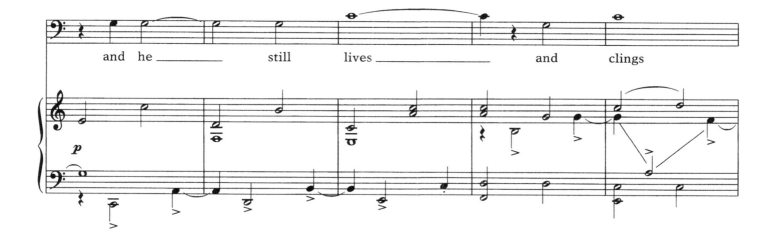

and he _____ still lives _____ and clings

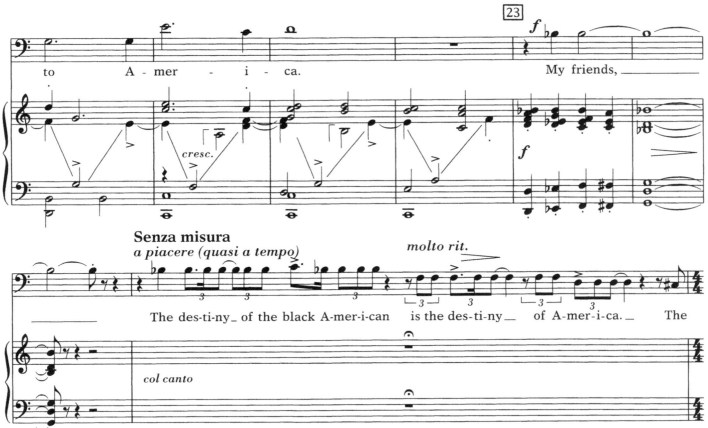

to A - mer - i - ca.

My friends, _____

Senza misura
a piacere (quasi a tempo)

molto rit.

col canto

_____ The des-ti-ny _ of the black A-mer-i-can is the des-ti-ny _ of A-mer-i-ca. _ The

24 *accel. molto*

Allegro (♩ = 132)

dim.

chain that binds the slave, _____

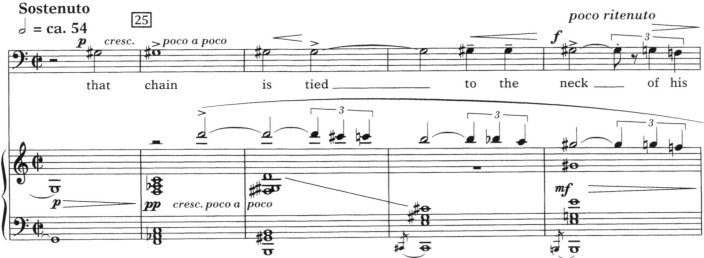

Sostenuto
♩ = ca. 54

25

poco ritenuto

that chain is tied _____ to the neck _____ of his

VI. Declaration

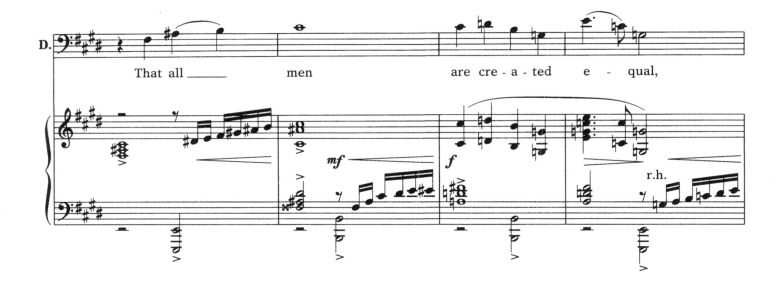

That all _____ men are cre - a - ted e - qual,

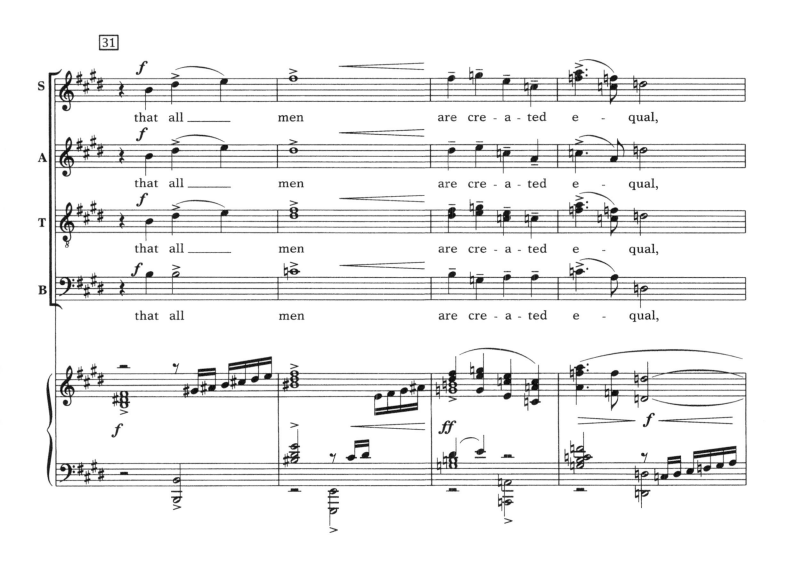

31

that all _____ men are cre - a - ted e - qual,

that all _____ men are cre - a - ted e - qual,

that all _____ men are cre - a - ted e - qual,

that all _____ men are cre - a - ted e - qual,

and the pur - suit _____ of

and the pur - suit of

and the pur - suit of

and the pur - suit of

34

ritenuto (in 4)

hap - pi-ness. _____

hap - - - pi - ness. _____

hap - - - pi - ness. _____

hap - - - pi - ness. _____

hap - - - pi - ness. _____

ritenuto (in 4)

cresc.